SPACE

KINGFISHER
LONDON & NEW YORK

Distributed in the U.S. and Canada by Macmillan,
175 Fifth Ave., New York, NY 10010

Library of Congress Cataloging-in-Publication data has been applied for.

Series editor: Hayley Down
Designer: Jeni Child

ISBN (PB): 978-0-7534-7350-4
ISBN (HB): 978-0-7534-7349-8

Kingfisher books are available for special promotions
and premiums. For details contact: Special Markets
Department, Macmillan, 175 Fifth Ave.,
New York, NY 10010.

For more information, please visit
www.kingfisherbooks.com

Printed in China

9 8 7 6 5 4 3 2 1

1TR/0417/WKT/UG/128MA

Picture credits
The Publisher would like to thank the following for permission to reproduce their material.
Top = t; Bottom = b; Middle = m; Left = l; Right = r
Front cover: NASA; Back cover: iStock/Creativemarc; Cover flap: Shutterstock/Egyptian Studio; Page 1 NASA/Hubble; 3 iStock/Ales_Utovko; 4–5, 4t, 4b, 5m NASA; 6 NASA/ESA/Hubble/Judy Schmidt; 7t Alamy/ Science Lab; 7m, 7b NASA; 8–9 Alamy/Iuliia Bycheva; 10–11 NASA; 12–13 Alamy/NASA Archive; 14–15 iStock/guvendemir; 15 Shutterstock/Quaoar; 16–17 NASA/JPL-Caltech/Cornell Univ./Arizona State Univ.; 16tr NASA/JPL; 16tm NASA/John Hopkins University Applied Physics Laboratory/Carnegie Institution of Washington; 16tml (Messenger) Creative Commons; 16tmr (Cassini) Creative Commons); 16bl NASA/ Johns Hopkins University Applied Physics Laboratory/Carnegie Institution of Washington and Dr Paolo C. Fienga/LXTT/IPF for the additional process and color; 16brNASA/JPL; 17tl, 17tr, 17bl NASA; 17br NASA/JPL/University of Arizona; 17tm Shutterstock/3Dsculptor; 18–19 NASA/JPL-Calt; 19tr NASA/JHUAPL; 19b NASA/University of Tennesee; 20tl, 20tr NASA; 20bl, 21tr, 21br, NASA/JPL; 20br NASA/JPL-Caltech/Space Science Institute; 21tl Lawrence Sromovsky, University of Wisconsin-Madison/W.W. Keck Observatory; 21bl Erich Karkoschka (University of Arizona) and NASA; 22 (1) Alamy/NASA/World History Archive & ARPL; 23tl (2), 23tl (3), 23mr (9), 23br (10) Creative Commons; 23ml (4) Shutterstock/Quaoar; 23bl (5) Alamy/World History Archive; 23bl (6), 23tr (8) NASA/JPL/Space Science Institute; 23tr (7) Alamy/World History Archive; 24 NASA; 25t Alamy/NASA Photo; 25m Creative Commons/European Southern Observatory (ESO); 25b NASA; 26–27 NASA, ESA, R. O'Connell (University of Virginia), F. Paresce (National Institute for Astrophysics, Bologna, Italy), E. Young (Universities Space Research Association/Ames Research Center), the WFC3 Science Oversight Committee, and the Hubble Heritage Team (STScI/AURA); 28–29 iStock/solarseven; 30–31 European Space Agency & NASA; 30 ESA/NASA; 31 ESA/Hubble and NASA; 32tr Shutterstock/NikitaRoytman Photography; 32bl NASA; 32br Alamy/Panther Media GmbH; 33bl Shutterstock/igordabari; 33br Alamy/Alan Dyer; 34 (1) NASA/CXC/JPL-Caltech/STScI; 35tl (2) Shutterstock/Egyptian Studio; 35tl (3) 35ml (4), 35bl (5), 35bl (6) 35tr (7), 35mr (9), NASA; 35tr (8) X-ray: NASA/CXC/Rutgers/J.Hughes; Optical: NASA/STScI; 35br (10) NASA/JPL-Caltech; 36tl, 37tl Credit: NASA, ESA, the Hubble Heritage Team (STScI/AURA), and R. Gendler (for the Hubble Heritage Team) Acknowledgment: J. GaBany; 36bl (Messier 101) NASA/JPL-Caltech/STScI; 36bl (Galaxy) ESA/Hubble & NASA and N. Gorin (STScI); 36br NASA/CXC/SAO; 37tr X-ray: NASA/CXC/MSU/J.Strader et al, Optical: NASA/STScI; 37br NASA/JPL-Caltech/SSC; 38 X-ray: NASA/CXC/Penn State/L.Townsley et al, Optical: ESO/2.2m telescope; 39t NASA; 39b iStock/ClaudioVentrella; 40–41 NASA/CXC/SAO/J. DePasquale; IR: NASA/JPL-Caltech; Optical: NASA/STScI; 42 iStock/den-belitsky; 43t NASA/JPL-Caltech/ESA/CXC/STScI; 43m NASA/ESO; 44, 45ml Shutterstock/pixelparticle; 45t NASA/JPL-Caltech/ESA/CXC/STScI; 45ml, 45m NASA/JPL-Caltech 46–47 NASA, ESA, and D. Coe, J. Anderson, and R. van der Marel (STScI); 47 NASA/JPL-Caltech; 48–49 NASA; 50 NASA; 51t, 51b NASA; 51m Getty/Corbis; 52 NASA/Bill Ingalls; 53t, 53b NASA; 54–55 NASA/JPL-Caltech/MSSS; 56 (1), 56mr (3), 56br (4), 57ml (5), 57bl (6), 57tr (7), 57mr (9), 59 br (10) NASA; 56bl (2) NASA/JPL-Caltech; 57tr (8) NASA Photo/Lori Losey; 58–59 Alamy/RGB Ventures; 58, 59 NASA; 60, 61, 62, NASA; 63 NASA/Hubble.

SPACE

BY **RAMAN PRINJA**
WITHDRAWN

KINGFISHER

NEW YORK

CONTENTS

ZOOM THROUGH SPACE

Space is the whole universe. We think of space as starting from above Earth's sky and stretching out beyond the Moon, planets, stars, and galaxies. The universe is incredibly vast, with powerful forces and huge energies at work inside it. In this book, we will zoom outward from Earth to explore objects that come into view as we move farther and farther out into space . . .

stars, gas, and dust in space

INSIDE YOU'LL FIND . . .

. . . the Solar System

ENERGY is the power needed to make things happen. You use energy to run or walk. Everything in space uses energy too! The Sun uses energy to shine, and the planets use energy to **orbit** the Sun.

COSMIC FACT

. . . spectacular stars and galaxies!

COSMIC FACT

Energy can be related to a **FORCE** that can cause movement by pushing or pulling. Gravity is a force that pulls things together. It holds stars together in groups called galaxies, which exist in many shapes and sizes.

. . . out-of-this-world explorers!

When measuring distances in space, astronomers use a measurement called a **LIGHT-YEAR**. It is the same as the distance light can travel through space in one year— it equals 9,500 billion kilometres. The Milky Way measures 150,000 light-years across.

COSMIC FACT

PLANETS

THE SOLAR SYSTEM

Venus

Mars

Mercury

Earth

Sun

asteroid belt

The solar system is about 4.6 billion years old. It is made up of the Sun and all the objects circling it along paths called orbits. The Sun is orbited by eight planets, hundreds of moons, millions of asteroids, several **dwarf planets**, and many space **probes** that people on Earth have sent into space.

You can remember the order of the planets using this sentence: "My Very Eager Mouse Just Swallowed Up Noodles." The first letter of each word will remind you of the first letter of the correct planet, starting from the Sun: Mercury, Venus, Earth, Mars, Jupiter, Saturn, Uranus, Neptune!

The **OORT CLOUD** is an icy shell that surrounds the **Kuiper Belt** and all the planets in the solar system. Astronomers think there may be two trillion cold comets in the Oort cloud.

Jupiter

Uranus

Saturn

Neptune

The **KUIPER BELT** is a region beyond Neptune that holds trillions of small, icy objects. It stretches up to 50 times the distance between Earth and the Sun. It is home to dwarf planets and comets.

The Sun contains 99.9 percent of the solar system's **MASS**, with Jupiter and Saturn making up most of the rest. Mercury, Venus, Earth, and Mars make up a tiny percentage of the solar system's mass.

CLOSE UP

PLANET EARTH

We live on a small, rocky planet called Earth, about 93 million mi. (150 million km) from our closest star, the Sun. Earth is very special because it is the only world known to support life. Almost 70 percent of Earth's surface is covered by its oceans of salty water.

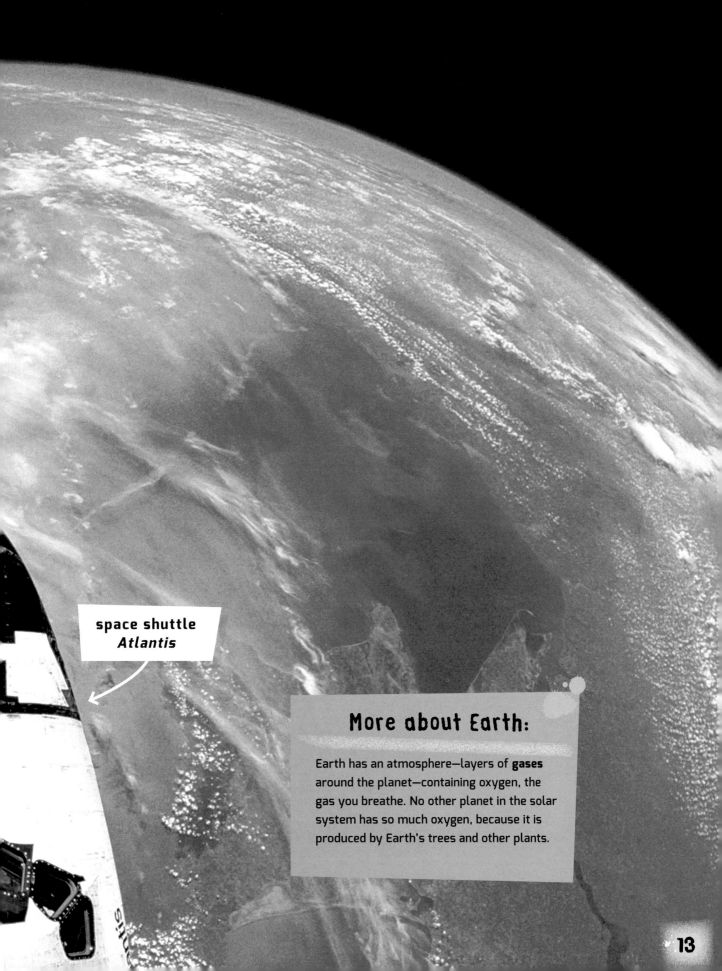

space shuttle
Atlantis

More about Earth:

Earth has an atmosphere—layers of **gases** around the planet—containing oxygen, the gas you breathe. No other planet in the solar system has so much oxygen, because it is produced by Earth's trees and other plants.

EARTH'S MOON

Your questions about the Moon answered.

How big is the Moon?

The Moon has a **diameter** of 2,159 mi. (3,475 km), which is about one-fourth of the size of Earth. If you imagine Earth as a basketball, then on this scale the Moon would be a tennis ball placed about 24.3 ft. (7.4 m) away.

How did the Moon form?

Scientists think the Moon was formed when a Mars-size object crashed into Earth about 4.5 billion years ago.
The smash threw material from Earth into orbit. Some of the material crashed back to Earth, but gravity squeezed the rest together to make the Moon. This idea is known as the giant-impact theory.

crater on the Moon

Why does the Moon change shape?

The Moon changes shape in our night sky. Sometimes we see it as a round disk, a half-circle, or even a banana-shaped crescent. The Moon is always ball-like in shape; what changes is how much of the sunlit part of the Moon we can see as it orbits Earth.

What is the Moon made of?

The Moon is covered in **craters**, dead volcanoes, and large areas where **lava** flowed billions of years ago. The inner parts of the Moon are made of rock and iron. The surface soil of the Moon is a fine, powdery material called regolith. Astronauts who walked on the Moon left footprints in this gray-colored soil!

Meet Earth's neighbors in the solar system! These relatively small planets are made mostly of rock and metal.

ROCKY

MESSENGER

Venus Express

MERCURY

Mercury is the closest planet to the Sun and is about the same size as Earth's Moon. Its surface is covered in deep, bowl-shaped craters. From day to night, the temperature can go from a scorching 806°F (430°C) to a freezing −305°F (−187°C). This is because the planet lacks an atmosphere to keep in the heat. Mercury is the solar system's fastest planet, orbiting the Sun at 107 mph (172 km/h). It has no moons.

craters on Mercury

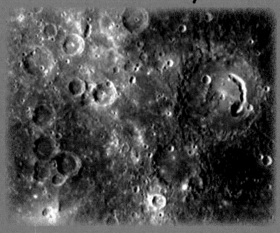

VENUS

The second planet from the Sun, Venus is Earth's "twin"—the two planets are about the same size! Venus is the brightest planet in our night sky. Its thick atmosphere is made mostly of carbon dioxide, with some clouds made of acid. The surface of Venus has many **extinct** volcanoes and lava flowed there billions of years ago. With a surface temperature of 864°F (462°C), Venus is the solar system's hottest planet. It has no moons.

volcano on Venus

PLANETS

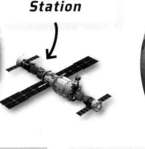

International Space Station

Curiosity

EARTH

Earth is the third planet from the Sun. Like Mercury and Venus, Earth has a rocky surface with mountains and deep canyons. Unlike other rocky planets, Earth has volcanoes that are still active today. Earth's **continents** sit on rocky plates that move to cause **earthquakes**. Earth is the only rocky planet in the solar system with oceans of water on its surface.

mountains on Earth

MARS

Mars is the farthest rocky planet from the Sun. It is sometimes known as the "Red Planet" because of the rusty iron material that covers its surface. Mars has the largest mountain in the solar system, known as Olympus Mons. At 13.7 mi. (22 km) tall, it is nearly three times taller than Mount Everest on Earth. The atmosphere of Mars is mostly made of carbon dioxide. Mars has two moons, called Phobos and Deimos.

frosted dunes on Mars

Billions of **ASTEROIDS** are found in a region between Mars and Jupiter called the asteroid belt.

CROSSING THE ASTEROID BELT

Asteroids are small, rocky objects that orbit the Sun. Studying asteroids can teach us how the planets formed.

The **ASTEROID BELT** is so vast that the distance between asteroids is on average 600,250 mi. (966,000 km). This means that spacecraft can fly through the asteroid belt without crashing into anything!

Asteroids are made of **ROCK**, **STONE**, and **METAL**. Some asteroids are very solid, while others are clumps of rubble loosely held together by gravity.

The **LARGEST** asteroid, Ceres, is 590 mi. (950 km) in diameter. It is also known as a dwarf planet.

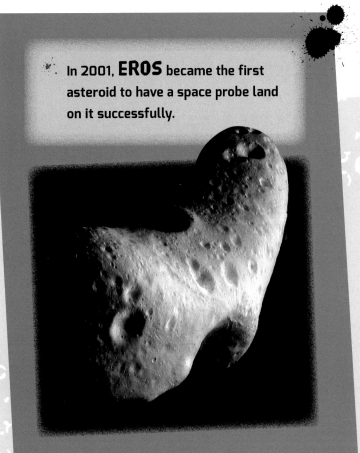

In 2001, **EROS** became the first asteroid to have a space probe land on it successfully.

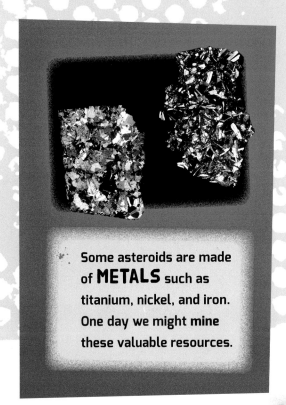

Some asteroids are made of **METALS** such as titanium, nickel, and iron. One day we might **mine** these valuable resources.

There are **200 OBJECTS** that are more than 62 mi. (100 km) in diameter in the asteroid belt, and almost one million asteroids that are more than 0.6 mi. (1 km) across.

In 2011, the **DAWN SPACECRAFT** became the first spacecraft to ever go into orbit around an asteroid in the asteroid belt.

The huge force of **JUPITER'S** gravity stopped objects in the asteroid belt from coming together to make a small planet.

The **TOTAL MASS** of the asteroid belt is less than that of Earth's Moon.

There is a huge jump in distance between Mars, the last rocky planet, and Jupiter, the first of the gas giants.

GIANT

JUPITER

Diameter: 88,846 mi. (142,984 km)
Mass: 318 Earths
Distance from Sun: 483.8 million mi. (778.6 million km)
Rings: 4 main
Moons: 67 known
Atmosphere: hydrogen, helium, methane
Rotation period: 9.9 hours
Temperature at top layers: −162°F (−108°C)

The Great Red Spot is a storm on Jupiter's surface; it is twice as wide as the Earth. In fact 1,321 planet Earths would fit inside Jupiter!

Jupiter's Great Red Spot

SATURN

Diameter: 74,898 mi. (120,536 km)
Mass: 95 Earths
Distance from Sun: 891 million mi. (1,434 million km)
Rings: more than 30
Moons: 62 known
Atmosphere: hydrogen, helium, methane
Rotation period: 10.7 hours
Temperature at top layers: 218°F (−139°C)

Saturn has storms that can last for six months, firing lightning bolts 10,000 times more powerful than those on Earth!

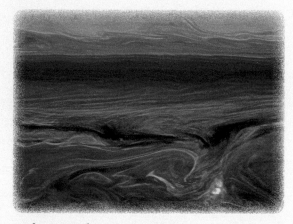

lightning storm on Saturn

GAS PLANETS

URANUS

Diameter: 31,763 mi. (51,118 km)
Mass: 15 Earths
Distance from Sun: 1.785 billion mi. (2,873 million km)
Rings: 13 main
Moons: 27 known
Atmosphere: hydrogen, helium, methane
Rotation period: 17.2 hours
Temperature at top layers: 323°F (–197°C)

The **poles** of Uranus are on its sides, not the top and bottom. This makes it look like the planet is rolling around the Sun on its side.

sideways Uranus

NEPTUNE

Diameter: 30,775 mi. (49,528 km)
Mass: 17 Earths
Distance from Sun: 2.793 billion mi. (4,495 million km)
Rings: 5 main
Moons: 14 known
Atmosphere: hydrogen, helium, methane
Rotation period: 16.1 hours
Temperature at top layers: 330°F (–201°C)

Neptune's atmosphere is made up of swirling clouds of a gas called methane. This gas gives the planet its bright blue color.

gassy Neptune!

MOONS

There are 181 known moons in the solar system, but which are the most interesting?

1

Io

Pronounced "eye-oh," this moon orbits Jupiter. Its surface is covered with hundreds of volcanoes, some of which erupt with such power that lava shoots dozens of miles into the air.

2 Triton

This is the only moon in the solar system to have a **retrograde orbit**—it orbits in the opposite direction to its planet's rotation.

7 Ganymede

This is the biggest moon in the solar system! Ganymede has oxygen in its atmosphere, but not enough for you to live there.

3 Phobos

Mars's largest moon is on a **collision course**! In 50 million years, it will crash into Mars or break up to form a ring. Look out!

8 Enceladus

One of Saturn's moons, Enceladus has a surface of ice that reflects light. An enormous ocean lies under this ice-crust.

4 Luna

"Luna" was the Roman name for Earth's Moon. We use "lunar" to describe things to do with the Moon, such as the lunar landing.

9 Europa

There is more water below the surface of Jupiter's moon Europa than there is in all of Earth's oceans put together.

5 Callisto

One of Jupiter's moons, Callisto has more craters than any other object in the solar system!

10 Titan

Saturn's largest moon has a thick atmosphere of gases. These gases give Titan its bright-orange color.

6 Iapetus

Iapetus, which orbits Saturn, is sometimes called the "yin and yang" moon. One side of its surface is very dark; the other is very light.

Which moon would you like to travel to?

DWARF PLANETS

In 2006, astronomers came up with a new term: dwarf planet. This is the name for an object that is smaller than a normal planet and ball-shaped, but is not a moon in orbit around another planet. Unlike a true planet, a dwarf planet's orbit around the Sun is littered with pieces of rock and other bodies.

COSMIC FACT

In addition to the eight main planets, there are five known **DWARF PLANETS** in the solar system. The dwarf planets are called Ceres, Pluto, Haumen, Makemake, and Eris. There may be hundreds more dwarf planets waiting to be discovered!

Ceres

Pluto

PLuTO is the largest known dwarf planet, with a diameter of 1,474 mi. (2,372 km). The smallest dwarf planet, Ceres, is 590 mi. (950 km) across.

Eris

The farthest dwarf planet from the Sun, **ERIS** takes 560 years to complete just one orbit around the Sun.

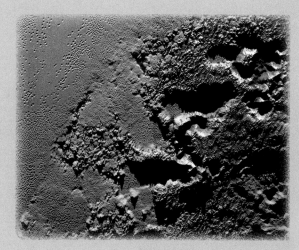

Pluto's surface

In July 2015, the NASA **SPACECRAFT** *New Horizons* made the first visit to Pluto. It sent us images of craters, cliffs, and valleys on Pluto's surface. It also sent close-ups of Pluto's five tiny moons!

STARS AND GALAXIES

THE SUN

The Sun is our closest star. Made of mostly hot hydrogen and helium gases, it provides Earth with the right amount of heat and light to make life possible. The Sun's mass gives it an enormous gravity, which keeps the planets of the solar system in orbit around it. The Sun's diameter is 870,000 mi. (1.4 million km); Earth would fit inside it more than one million times! Light takes 8 minutes to travel from the Sun to Earth.

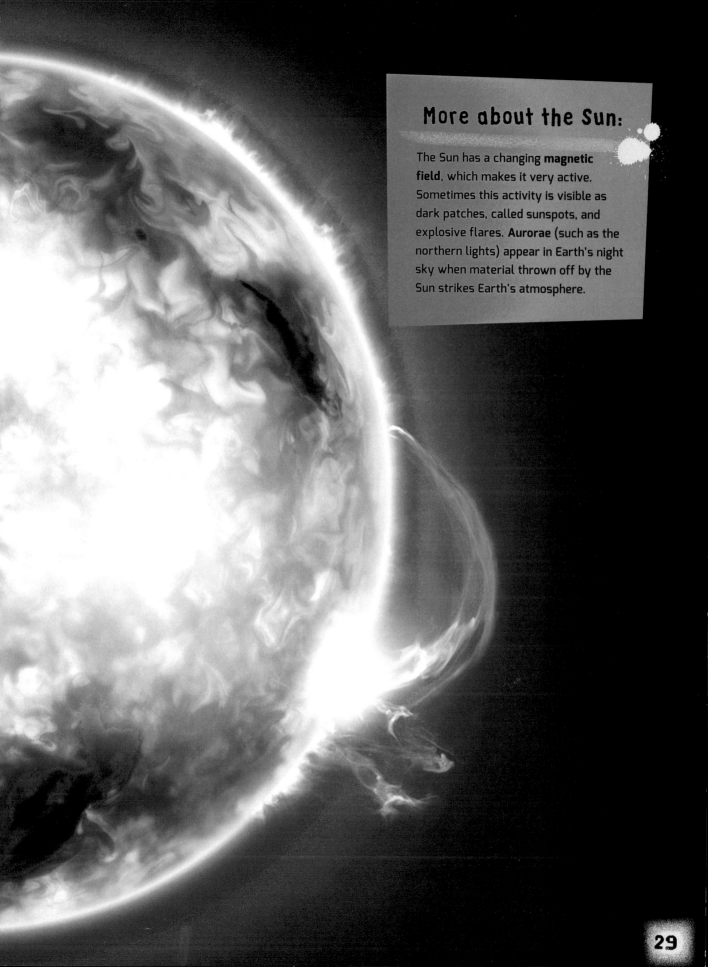

The Sun has a changing **magnetic field**, which makes it very active. Sometimes this activity is visible as dark patches, called sunspots, and explosive flares. **Aurorae** (such as the northern lights) appear in Earth's night sky when material thrown off by the Sun strikes Earth's atmosphere.

STELLAR NIGHT SKY

Your questions about spectacular stars answered!

Why do stars twinkle?

Stars twinkle because the air in Earth's atmosphere is moving around. This movement is called turbulence. The shifting air bends the light's path as it travels from a star to our eyes. From outside our atmosphere, a star's shine is constant, not twinkly!

Why are stars different colors?

If you look carefully, you should see that stars in the night sky are not all the same color. There are some reddish, orange, and blue stars, along with many white and yellow ones. The stars have different colors because their outer layers (the photospheres) have different temperatures. Red stars are cooler than blue ones.

Why are some stars brighter than others?

There are bright and dim stars because some stars are much closer to Earth than others, making them appear much brighter. Stars also have different brightnesses because some of them are more powerful and give off a lot more light. Older stars may become small and dim.

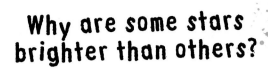

Where do the stars go during the day?

During daytime, the stars *are* still in the sky! You cannot see them because the light from the Sun is so bright. Sunlight is spread across our sky by Earth's atmosphere, making it too bright to see the fainter stars in the sky.

CONSTELLATIONS

AQUILA: THE EAGLE

Aquila is easiest to spot during the summer in the Northern **Hemisphere**. In Greek mythology Aquila, "the Eagle," served the god Zeus, sending messages down to Earth. Zeus was so pleased with Aquila's actions that he placed the Eagle among the stars to fly forever through the sky.

CASSIOPEIA: THE QUEEN

Cassiopeia is an easy constellation to look for in the autumn skies of the Northern Hemisphere. In ancient myths, Cassiopeia was a queen known for her great beauty. However, she was punished for boasting about how beautiful she was, and so the gods forced Cassiopeia to remain in the sky tied to a chair.

Constellations are patterns drawn using the stars—like connect-the-dot puzzles! Ancient people named them after characters from their myths and legends. Today, astronomers use 88 constellations to map the night sky.

CYGNUS: THE SWAN

Cygnus is one of the brightest constellations. It can be seen from June to December in the Northern Hemisphere and in the winter months in the Southern Hemisphere. One ancient Greek myth says that Zeus once disguised himself as a swan to take Queen Leda under his wings and save her when she was attacked by an eagle.

ORION: THE HUNTER

Orion is a great constellation to look out for in the Northern Hemisphere from November to February. Two of the brightest 10 stars in the night sky, Rigel and Betelgeuse, are in this constellation. In Greek mythology, Orion was a great hunter and the son of Poseidon, the sea god. He hunted to provide the gods with food.

TOP 10

STAR STAGES

Stars don't live forever! They have life-cycles that last billions of years.

1 A star in the making

Stars are born in clouds called nebulae, made mostly of hydrogen and helium gases.

A star is born

Inside a nebula, matter is squeezed tightly by gravity, becoming very hot. This forms the star.

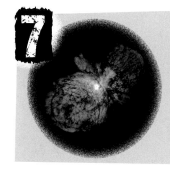

Massive stars

Stars that are born with much more mass than the Sun have a much shorter life-cycle. They are called massive stars.

Long lives

Stars live for ages! The Sun will last for about 10 billion years. It is currently halfway through its life-cycle.

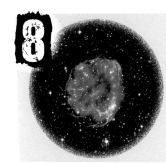

Supernovae

Massive stars die in explosions called supernovae.

Out of energy

All stars die when their supply of **nuclear energy** runs out and they cannot shine anymore.

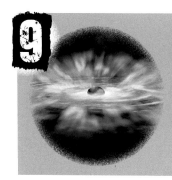

Black holes

A supernova can leave behind a very strange thing: a black hole! Its gravity is so strong that even light cannot escape it.

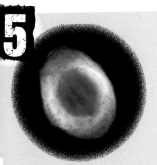

Planetary nebulae

About five billion years from now, the Sun will die by throwing out gas to make a **planetary nebula**.

New stars

The matter thrown out in a supernova explosion spreads out in space and may be recycled to make new stars.

White dwarfs

The final stage in a star's death will come when it is squeezed by gravity to make an Earth-size star, called a white dwarf.

Which star stage is the most fascinating?

Galaxy M106

GALAXY

A galaxy is a group of billions of stars and clouds of gas and dust held together by gravity. Our solar system is in a galaxy called the Milky Way. There are four main types of galaxy . .

SPIRAL

A spiral galaxy looks like a pinwheel. The central part of the galaxy is a large bulge of many tightly packed stars. Arms made of young stars and dust spiral outward from the bulge. Our Milky Way galaxy is a spiral galaxy. This type of galaxy contains many young and old stars.

Messier 101

ELLIPTICAL

Elliptical galaxies are oval or egg-shaped. They don't have arms. These galaxies contain mostly very old stars, and not many new stars are being made inside them. Some of the largest galaxies in the universe are elliptical. They can span one million light-years across.

Centaurus A

TYPES

Sombrero

NGC 4649

LENTICULAR

A lenticular galaxy is midway between a spiral and an elliptical galaxy. It has an egg-shaped bulge in the middle and very faint arms that are tightly wound around its center. These galaxies are normally much brighter than spiral galaxies.

IRREGULAR

Irregular galaxies have no clear shape or pattern. They are small galaxies with many clouds of gas and dust inside them. A lot of new stars are being made in irregular galaxies. This can make the galaxies very bright.

IC 1613

MRK 820

Clouds of gas and dust in the Sagittarius spiral arm of the Milky Way galaxy

The Milky Way Galaxy is an incredible **13.5 BILLION** years old.

OUR MILKY WAY GALAXY

Find out incredible facts about our home galaxy!

- There is a supermassive **BLACK HOLE** at the center of our galaxy. The black hole has a mass of about four million Suns!

- The Milky Way galaxy is very flat. It is **100,000** light-years in diameter, but only a few thousand light-years thick.

The Milky Way galaxy is made up of **200 BILLION** stars!

- The galaxy is surrounded by a halo, which contains a mysterious type of **matter**, called **DARK MATTER**. You cannot directly see dark matter through a telescope.

The **MILKY WAY** gets its name from a fuzzy white band of stars that you can see stretching across the sky at night. This is our view of it from inside the galaxy.

COLLIDING GALAXIES

Sometimes galaxies can be squeezed so close together that they crash into each other! In this image from the Hubble Space Telescope, you can see two spiral galaxies, called NGC 4038 and NGC 4039, colliding. They are about 45 million light-years away from Earth.

NGC 4038

NGC 4039

More about galaxies:

Billions of years from now, the galaxies will have **merged** to make one new supergalaxy, with many bright new stars!

GALAXY GROUPS

A galaxy group is a collection of a few dozen galaxies, brought together by gravity into an area that measures a few million light-years across.

The Milky Way belongs to the Local Group, which contains about 50 galaxies crowded together into a space with a diameter of 10 million light-years!

The Arp 273 grouping of galaxies is about 300 million light-years away from Earth.

GALAXY CLUSTERS are **LARGER** structures containing a few hundred galaxies packed into a region that measures a few million light-years across. The Local Group is brought together with other galaxy groups to make a galaxy cluster called Virgo.

galaxies in Virgo cluster

supercluster

SUPERCLUSTERS are even larger collections of galaxies! They can extend over a few hundred million light-years and bring together many clusters. The Virgo cluster is found inside a supercluster called **LANIAKEA**.

Your home address may be written as follows: street address, town or city, state, zip code, country, continent. Now you can write your address in the universe too! Here it is:

PLANET EARTH, SOLAR SYSTEM, MILKY WAY GALAXY, LOCAL GROUP, VIRGO CLUSTER, LANIAKEA SUPERCLUSTER

THE BIG BANG

Most scientists believe the universe was born about 13.8 billion years ago in an incredibly large explosion of energy called the big bang. In a very tiny fraction of a second, a huge amount of energy was produced. At this time, the universe was very small and extremely hot. Time, space, and matter all began with the big bang.

COSMIC FACT

In just a fraction of a second after the big bang, the universe **GREW** in size from smaller than a single atom to bigger than a galaxy!

the big bang

early stars

When the universe was **ONE SECOND** old, tiny particles began to form. After three minutes, the universe was cool enough for the particles to come together to make the centers of atoms. About 380,000 years later, the universe cooled enough for complete atoms to form. All matter in the universe is made up of atoms. The first stars were made 100 million years after the big bang.

how the universe grows

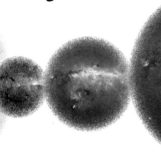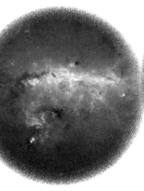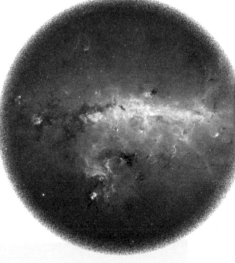

The universe **GREW RAPIDLY** after the big bang and has kept on growing at an amazing rate. It is still expanding (getting bigger) today. You can think of the expanding universe as a little like blowing up a balloon. All of the galaxies that formed would be like dots drawn on the balloon, and they are all moving away from each other as the balloon gets larger and larger.

THE END?

Your questions about the end of the universe answered!

What is the big rip?

The big rip **model** suggests that a mysterious type of energy, called dark energy, takes over and pushes the universe apart very rapidly. This energy acts against gravity and tears apart all of the galaxies and stars.

Do we know how the universe will end?

Scientists are not sure exactly how the universe will change in the future. They are studying how much mass and energy exist in the universe. This will help them understand whether the universe will keep expanding forever or if it might collapse on itself. There are a few possible ways the universe might end . . .

What is the big crunch?

In the big crunch model, the universe stops expanding and then starts to contract (get smaller). As the universe shrinks, all of the galaxies are crushed back together. At the end, all matter in the universe will collapse into the biggest black hole ever!

What is the big freeze?

Another possibility is that the universe will keep slowly expanding forever. All matter, such as galaxies, will be pushed farther apart. Slowly, all of the heat of the universe will spread very thinly across space. In the end, everything will become very cold and dark.

EXPLORING
SPACE

EYES ON THE UNIVERSE

The universe is incredibly vast, and the stars and galaxies are very far away. This means that the light reaching us from objects in space is very faint, just the way the headlights of a car would be very dim at night if the car was far away from you. To learn about galaxies, stars, and planets, astronomers collect the light from them using large telescopes.

COSMIC FACT

The **HUBBLE SPACE TELESCOPE** is one of the most successful telescopes ever. It is in orbit about 367 mi. (590 km) above Earth. Working above the atmosphere, it has a much clearer view of the universe.

Hubble
Space
Telescope

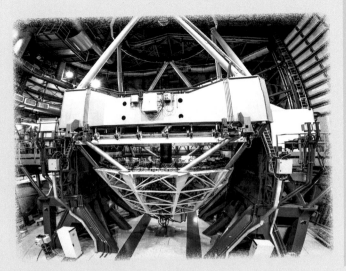

mirror telescope

Most telescopes use light-collecting **MIRRORS** to act as eyes on the universe. The bigger the telescope, the more light is collected, making the image a lot clearer. Astronomers use giant telescopes with mirrors that are many feet in diameter.

The 33 ft. (10 m)-wide **KECK** telescopes in Hawaii are so powerful that they could detect a light as small as the flame of a candle placed at a distance as far away as the Moon!

Keck telescope

VLT

The **VLT**s (Very Large Telescopes) in Chile allow astronomers to view objects that are four billion times fainter than we can see with our eyes alone.

NASA's latest mission to Jupiter is called **JUNO**. It was launched in 2011 aboard a powerful *Atlas V* rocket and arrived at the planet in 2016.

MISSIONS
TO THE PLANETS

Amazing discoveries have been made by sending spacecraft to explore the solar system. Here are some fantastic missions:

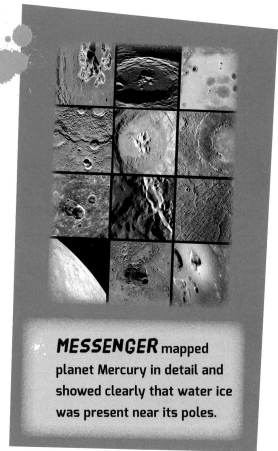

MESSENGER mapped planet Mercury in detail and showed clearly that water ice was present near its poles.

- In July 2015, NASA's **NEW HORIZONS** spacecraft made the very first visit to the dwarf planet Pluto. It took more than nine years to travel the 3 billion mi. (4.8 billion km) to reach the planet.

- Launched in March 2004 by the European Space Agency, the **ROSETTA** mission was flown to a comet called 67P/Churyumov Gerasimenko. In August 2014, the spacecraft went into orbit around the comet. It even landed a probe to explore the comet's rugged surface.

- **MESSENGER** was the first spacecraft ever to orbit the innermost planet Mercury. It arrived at the rocky planet on March 17, 2011. To end the mission on April 30, 2015, the spacecraft was deliberately slammed into the surface of the planet, carving out a small new crater.

- Orbiting Jupiter, **JUNO** has beamed back photos of violent storms swirling around the planet's north and south poles.

NEW HORIZONS sent back close-ups of valleys and cliffs on Pluto's surface. We also got views of Pluto's five tiny moons!

ROAMING AROUND MARS

Curiosity is like a moving laboratory, full of scientific experiments. It has 17 cameras, and a scoop to gather and study dust. It even has a laser and drill to blast rocks and see what they are made of! The information beamed back by *Curiosity* is helping scientists learn about whether Mars could have supported life forms in the past . . . or even today!

CLOSE UP

More about Curiosity:

This is a "selfie" of NASA's *Curiosity* rover on the surface of Mars. *Curiosity* is a car-size vehicle that arrived on Mars in August 2012. It is controlled remotely from Earth and has been exploring the planet for the past few years.

TOP 10

SPACE
MISSIONS

Discover the top 10 space
exploration missions so far!

1 Space walks

In 2001, astronauts Jim Voss and Susan Helms spent the longest time working on a space walk. They spent 8 hours and 56 minutes working outside the International Space Station.

2 Voyager 1

The most distant spacecraft from us is *Voyager 1*. It is now traveling in **interstellar space**, almost 12 billion mi. (19 billion km) away.

3 Odyssey

The longest working orbiting spacecraft is *Odyssey*. It has completed more than 60,000 orbits around Mars.

4 Opportunity

Opportunity is the longest-surviving rover. It has been traveling and working on the surface of Mars since January 2005.

Apollo 17

7

Astronauts Eugene Cernan and Harrison Schmitt spent the longest time on the Moon: 22 hours, 5 minutes, and 4 seconds.

Discovery

8

The most used spacecraft is space shuttle *Discovery*. It launched the Hubble Telescope and helped to build the *International Space Station*. Wow!

Saturn V

9

NASA's *Saturn V* type of rocket is the most powerful rocket used so far. It was used to launch the Apollo missions to the Moon.

Hayabusa

5

Japan's *Hayabusa* was the first spacecraft to collect dust from an asteroid and return it to Earth.

ISS

10

The International Space Station is the largest structure humans have ever put into space. It is almost 360 ft. (110 m) wide!

Juno

6

The fastest spacecraft is *Juno*, which whizzed toward Jupiter at 165,000 mph (265,500 km/h). It used engines and the pull of gravity.

Where in space would you like to explore?

INTERNATIONAL SPACE STATION

Your questions about life aboard the *ISS* answered!

What is the ISS?

The *International Space Station* (*ISS*) is a space laboratory that is in low orbit around Earth. Astronauts from around the world live and work there. The *ISS* is powered by enormous solar arrays (solar panels), which produce enough energy to power 40 homes on Earth.

What do astronauts eat in space?

Space food has come in many forms over the years, from squeezable tubes of liquid to cubes of dried food. Now, it usually comes premade in packets—a little like camping food—that can be warmed up in the *ISS* oven. There is a huge menu, with 72 types of food to choose from!

What do astronauts do on the *ISS*?

Astronauts go to the *ISS* to conduct experiments, carry out research, and make repairs. In their spare time, they can watch movies, read, and phone their family. There is even gym equipment so they can stay fit!

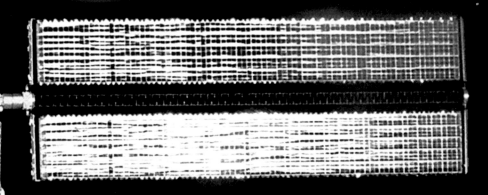

How do astronauts train for the ISS?

Astronauts train hard before shooting into space! They prepare for microgravity in water tanks; they practice living in cramped conditions; and they even have language lessons so they can speak to the Russian Mission Control Center!

International Space Station

THE SUPER SPACE QUIZ

Are you an expert on all things space? Test your knowledge by completing this quiz! When you've answered all of the questions, turn to page 63 to check your score.

 1 Name the telescope that is in orbit around Earth.
a) Bubble
b) Hubble
c) Trouble

 2 What does *ISS* stand for?
a) *International Space Station*
b) *International Space Stop*
c) *International Solar Spot*

 3 What is it called when an astronaut leaves the *ISS* to work outside in open space?
a) Space walk
b) Space wander
c) Space stroll

 4 How old is the solar system?
a) 4.6 thousand years
b) 4.6 million years
c) 4.6 billion years

 5 Which is the only planet that is known to have life on it?
a) Mars
b) Earth
c) Pluto

 6 If you imagine Earth as a basketball, which sports ball would the Moon be on this scale?
a) Tennis ball
b) Volleyball
c) Ping-pong ball

 7 What are stars made of?
a) Mostly hydrogen and helium gases
b) Mostly lava
c) Mostly rock and ice

 8 A red star seen in the night sky is . . .
a) cooler than a blue star
b) hotter than a blue star
c) the same temperature as a blue star

 9 How long is the life cycle of the Sun?
a) 1 million years
b) 10 million years
c) 10 billion years

How many Earths would fit inside Jupiter?
a) 103
b) 1,321
c) 1 million

 How many dwarf planets are currently known in the solar system?
a) 1
b) 3
c) 5

 Where do we find most of the comets in the solar system?
a) Oort cloud
b) Sort cloud
c) Port cloud

 How long does it take light to travel from the Sun to Earth?
a) 8 minutes
b) 6 minutes
c) 4 minutes

 What type of galaxy is our Milky Way galaxy?
a) Spiral
b) Elliptical
c) Irregular

 How many stars are there in our galaxy?
a) 200 billion
b) 20 billion
c) 2 billion

 What type of object is found at the center of our galaxy?
a) A supermassive black hole
b) A star
c) A wormhole

 What is happening to the two galaxies called NGC 4038 and NGC 4039?
a) They are crashing into each other
b) They are moving away from each other
c) They are orbiting each other

 How old is the universe?
a) 13.8 billion years
b) 12 billion years
c) 11 billion years

 The universe today is . . .
a) Contracting
b) Expanding
c) Staying still

 What is the name of a universe where everything collapses and gets squeezed together in the future?
a) The big crunch
b) The big hunch
ßc) The big lunch

GLOSSARY

atom
A tiny particle. Everthing in the universe is made up of atoms.

aurora
A display of colored light seen in the sky when particles from the Sun enter the Earth's atmosphere.

collision course
When two bodies in space are going to crash into each other.

continent
A large mass of land. Earth's continents are: Africa, Antarctica, Asia, Europe, North America, Oceania, and South America.

crater
A bowl-shaped hole made by an object from space hitting the surface of a planet or moon.

diameter
The length of a straight line passing through the center of a circle. The line connects two points on the edge of the circle.

dwarf planet
A ball-shaped object that is smaller than a normal planet, but is not a moon in orbit around another planet.

earthquake
A violent shaking felt on Earth's surface, caused by sudden movements of its continents.

extinct (volcano)
No longer erupting and not likely to do so in the future.

gas
A type of matter that is not liquid or solid. The air you breathe is made of gases.

gravity
The force that attracts bodies toward each other. The greater a body's mass, the greater its pull of gravity.

hemisphere
The half of Earth (or planet) between the north or south pole and the equator.

interstellar space
The gas and dust that exist in the space between the stars.

Kuiper Belt
A large ring of icy objects in our Solar System, beyond Neptune.

lava
Hot, molten rock that erupts onto the surface of a planet and starts to flow.

magnetic field
The lines of force that surround a permanent magnet or moving electric particles.

merged
When two bodies (such as galaxies) come together and make a new, more massive body.

mine
To dig out coal, metals, and other natural materials from the surface of a planet or other space body.

model
A scientific idea about how something works.

nuclear energy
Energy released from the center of an atom

planetary nebula
A cloud of gas seen surrounding Sun-like stars when they begin to die.

pole
The point at either end of the invisible line known as the axis, around which a planet spins.

probe
A spacecraft that explores space.

retrograde orbit
The path of an object in a clockwise direction when viewed from an imaginary point above the solar system.

QUIZ ANSWERS: 1 = b, 2 = a, 3 = a, 4 = c, 5 = b, 6 = a, 7 = a, 8 = a, 9 = c, 10 = b, 11 = c, 12 = a, 13 = a, 14 = a, 15 = a, 16 = a, 17 = a, 18 = a, 19 = b, 20 = a.

INDEX